FIND
TUTANKHAMEN
AND HIS TOMB

THE GREAT DISCOVERY
BY HOWARD CARTER
& GEORGE HERBERT

By

G. ELLIOT SMITH

First published in 1923

Read &' Co.

Copyright © 2022 Read & Co. History

This edition is published by Read & Co. History,
an imprint of Read & Co.

This book is copyright and may not be reproduced or copied in any
way without the express permission of the publisher in writing.

British Library Cataloguing-in-Publication Data
A catalogue record for this book is available
from the British Library.

Read & Co. is part of Read Books Ltd.
For more information visit
www.readandcobooks.co.uk

CONTENTS

ILLUSTRATIONS

THE ROMANCE
OF EXCAVATION

An Excerpt by David Masters

WHEN Professor Flinders Petrie first set foot in Egypt he was a young man, only twenty-seven years of age. The older men of other nations who had spent their lives delving in the past smiled at the idea of the new-comer bringing about a revolution in the work they knew so well. They had done so much themselves that there seemed little more for him to do. They had found tombs and statues and papyri that took them back some five thousand years to what they thought was the beginning of Egyptian history.

What else was there to discover?

Nobody knew then. Nobody knows now. When men start digging up the earth in search of relics of the past, it is beyond human foresight to foretell what will come to light. Men may dig 50 feet and find nothing. They may say there is nothing to be found in that particular spot. Another man may come along, set up his tent a few yards away, just scratch the surface of the soil, and find a buried city. This is what lures men to the work; it is one of the fascinations and provides much of the romance.

The wonderful discovery of the tomb of King Tutankhamen by Lord Carnarvon and Mr. Howard Carter is a notable instance of this sort of thing. For years they dug, poured money into the sands of the desert, shifting mountains of sand and rock in their endeavours to discover something worth while. Lord Carnarvon himself stated that they had moved about 70,000 tons of rubble during their search. They were lucky to be rewarded in the end, for millions of tons of rock and sand have been dug up in Egypt without yielding to the diggers a single article of value.

Mr. Howard Carter was hopeful that something might be found in the neighbourhood of the great discovery, and the work of excavation was started. The diggers wielded their picks week after week and shovelled the rubble into the baskets of the men who carried it away from the hole that was growing in the ground. Daily the hole grew bigger, the mound of sand and rock grew larger.

Not a sign of a tomb was discovered. Work was continued in the hope that something would turn up. They were always hopeful, but the end of the day brought nothing to light and it proved so much wasted labour.

The quest in the old place was thrown up, and the picks of the diggers were directed to a spot only a few yards away. There was the same monotonous, back-aching work, the same running to and fro of the natives with their little baskets of rubble. In such circumstances, only a born optimist could carry on. The pessimist would throw up the task in despair at the end of two or three days.

Even Mr. Howard Carter began to think that he had again drawn a blank; he began to consider whether it was time to shut down operations and have another try elsewhere. For a day or two his thoughts ran in this groove, until he decided to dig just one more day, and if nothing turned up then to stop it.

Truly a momentous decision. But for it the tomb of Tutankhamen would still be undiscovered, and the world would yet be in ignorance of the marvels that it contained. Before the day's digging was over, the shape of a step gladdened Mr. Carter's eyes, and fully justified his selection of that particular spot for his operations. A yard or two more to the right or left, and he might have missed the tomb. It was a much nearer thing than the world imagines.

The accuracy of Mr. Howard Carter in selecting his second site is rather amazing. Digging was not started there haphazard.

The ground had been thoroughly gone over and studied, and the possibilities summed up before the pick was driven into the sand. It was a happy combination of expert knowledge and good luck.

It at once became obvious why the tomb had remained for so long undiscovered, for just above it the last resting-place of Thothmes III was cut into the rock, and all the debris from this later tomb had been shot by the builders on top of the earlier tomb. This rubbish had completely covered in the site of the tomb of Tutankhamen and buried it for centuries.

Few men would think of looking immediately under one tomb for the site of another. Such a place is so unexpected that Mr. Howard Carter deserved every credit for selecting so unlikely a spot in which to carry on his search.

AN EXCERPT FROM
The Romance of Excavation, 1923

PREFACE

During the period when the newspapers were publishing daily reports of the progress of the work in Tutankhamen's tomb and Mr Harry Burton's photographs, which gave us so vivid an impression of the objects that were being found, I wrote for the *Daily Telegraph* a series of articles discussing the wider significance of the startling discoveries. They did not describe the tomb itself or the wonderful collection of funerary equipment, but were merely a general commentary on the meaning of the information being given by the reporters from the Theban necropolis. Nor was any attempt made to collect the few facts concerning Tutankhamen himself, or even to discuss the events of his time. The exploration of the Valley of the Tombs of the Kings, for which the late Lord Carnarvon and Mr Howard Carter were responsible, had brought to light the tomb of the youthful nonentity Tutankhamen, which sheds a dazzling searchlight on one particular phase of the history of civilization thirty centuries ago. What I set out to attempt was to interpret the deeper meaning of those Egyptian beliefs which found such brilliant expression in the luxuriously extravagant equipment of his tomb.

I have been urged to collect these articles into the more convenient form of this little book. As they were merely comments on the descriptions of the actual tomb and its contents the separate issue of these topical and ephemeral notes seemed at first to lack any justification, but I have received so many requests for information and guidance that I thought it might serve some useful purpose to redraft my articles and give such bibliographical references as would help the general reader to understand the results that have so far been attained and to appreciate the value of the more important discoveries that next season's work will certainly reveal.

I have used the pharaoh's name "Tutankhamen" as the title of this book merely as a label to suggest the circumstance that called it into being. But I have written an introductory chapter to give an account of what is known of him and his times.

BIBLIOGRAPHICAL NOTE

The only accurate and reliable account that has ever been given of the Egyptian funerary practices and their significance is Dr Alan Gardiner's introductory memoir on *The Tomb of Amenemhēt* (illustrated by Nina de Garis Davies) which was published in 1915 under the auspices of the Egypt Exploration Fund (now Society).

Dr Gardiner describes the actual condition of affairs found in a private Theban tomb of the eighteenth dynasty (in the reign of Thothmes III, about a century earlier than Tutankhamen); and in the light of his intimate knowledge and understanding of the literature of the period, he interprets the meaning of the arrangement of the tomb and especially of the scenes and inscriptions sculptured and painted upon the walls, which Mrs de Garis Davies has reproduced with such skill and accuracy. This unique work is indispensable to anyone who wants to read what the ancient Egyptians themselves actually wrote to express their beliefs or interpret their customs. Professor James H. Breasted's *History of Egypt* and *Development of Religion and Thought in Ancient Egypt* are the best guides to a knowledge of the history and religion of ancient Egypt. The late Sir Gaston Maspero's *Egyptian Art* (London, 1913) contains a great deal of information directly relevant to the interpretation of objects in Tutankhamen's tomb. But Mr Burton's photographs of Tutankhamen's funerary equipment give a new interest and value to Birch's edition of Sir Gardner Wilkinson's *The Manners and Customs of the Ancient Egyptians* (London, 1878), for many of the objects and funeral scenes depicted in that remarkable book enable us to form a mental picture of the Valley of the Tombs as the funeral of Tutankhamen wound its way to the place where Mr Howard Carter has just brought to light so many articles closely analogous to those depicted in Birch's and Wilkinson's book.

All the information at present available concerning the life of Tutankhamen and Horemheb, his successor once removed, was collected and published (in 1912) by the late Sir Gaston Maspero, *The Tombs of Harmhabi and Touatânkhamanou* (*Theodore M. Davis' Excavations*).

The other volumes of reports published by Mr Theodore Davis are valuable for reference and comparison in studying the results of the exploration of Tutankhamen's tomb. The two volumes, *The Tomb of Iouiya and Touiyou* (1907) and *The Tomb of Queen Tiyi* (1910) are specially important, and relevant to the discoveries in Tutankhamen's tomb. Mr Arthur Weigall's book *The Life and Times of Akhnaton* gives a popular and romantic picture of his conception of the history of the times of Tutankhamen and his father-in-law.

FINDING TUTANKHAMEN AND HIS TOMB

CHAPTER I

INTRODUCTORY

Never before in the history of archæological inquiry has any event excited such immediate and world-wide interest as Mr Howard Carter's discovery of Tutankhamen's tomb in November 1922. Very little is known as yet of the king himself, but twelve months hence no doubt his mummy will give up its secrets and perhaps the story of his life will be revealed. But at the moment he is supposed to have been merely a colourless youth, who reigned for a few years only, and achieved such notoriety as is associated with his name by virtue of weakness rather than strength of character. For his religious and political opinions seem to have been as plastic as those of the famous Vicar of Bray, adapting themselves with facility to his changing environment. The objects so far found in his tomb do not add very materially to our knowledge of history.

Yet, in spite of the unimportance of Tutankhamen himself and the comparative lack of new historical data, the world-wide interest the discovery has evoked is amply warranted by the new appreciation of historical values it affords.

It gives us a new revelation of the wealth and luxury of

Egyptian civilization during its most magnificent period. The value of the gold and precious objects far surpasses that of any hoard previously recovered from ancient times. Judged merely by its quantity the collection of furniture is the most wonderful ever found; and everyone who has examined the individual pieces agrees that in beauty of design and perfection of craftsmanship Tutankhamen's funerary equipment is indeed a new revelation of the ancient Egyptians' artistic feeling and technical skill, far surpassing anything known before.

The fact that the tomb of so insignificant a personage as Tutankhamen was equipped with such lavish magnificence adds to the importance of the discovery. For if a youthful nonentity who reigned no more than six or seven years in one of the leanest phases of Egypt's history had all this wealth poured into his tomb, one's imagination tries in vain to picture the funerary equipment of the famous and longer-lived pharaohs, such as Thothmes III, who established the Egyptian Empire in Asia and could command the tribute of the then civilized world, or Amenhotep III, under whom the sovereign power in Egypt attained its culmination, and luxury and ostentation their fullest expression. Or again what riches must have been poured into the vast tombs of Seti I and Rameses II, the powerful pharaohs who recovered for a time the Egyptian dominion in Asia which Akhenaton and his sons-in-law had lost? A thousand years before Christ the desolate Valley of the Tombs of the Kings must have had buried in its recesses the vastest collection of gold and precious furniture that perhaps was ever collected in one spot in the history of the world. For these reasons alone there is ample justification for the world-wide interest in the discovery which will always be associated with the names of Lord Carnarvon and Mr Howard Carter.

But apart from its interest as an artistic revelation and the intrinsic value of the objects found the discovery is important for other reasons. The dazzling display of skill and luxury has forced the scholar and the man in the street to recognize in some

16

measure the vastness of the achievements of ancient Egyptian civilization and to ask themselves whether this vigorous and highly developed culture could have failed to exert a much more profound influence upon its neighbours than is generally admitted. When it is recalled that Egypt herself devised the ships and developed the seamanship which created the chief bond of union with Syria and Crete, East Africa and Arabia, the Persian Gulf and beyond, we should be in a better position to realize the plain meaning of the evidence that points to Egypt as the dominating factor in shaping the nascent civilization of the world. The wide interest in the revelation of Egypt's achievements more than thirty centuries ago should prepare men's minds impartially to study the vast significance of the facts thus displayed by Mr Howard Carter's investigations.

Besides revealing the wonderful equipment of a royal tomb the discovery of Tutankhamen's tomb enables us to examine many objects and articles of funerary equipment hitherto known to us only in pictures. This makes it possible for us not only to study and appreciate the nature of the things themselves, but also to acquire new confidence in the accuracy and the reality of the scenes and the objects depicted upon the walls of the tombs and the pictures inscribed on papyri. Many of the illustrations that have long been familiar to us in the old books of Belzoni, Lepsius, Rosellini, and Wilkinson, have acquired a new meaning and a new reality from the discovery of Tutankhamen's tomb. Moreover, when the examination of the tomb is completed, and we learn something of the mummy, the king's distinctive features, his age, and his ailments, we shall be able to read the history of his time more clearly, and perhaps be able to appreciate the deeper significance of one of the most piquant phases in the history of civilization.

At the time of Tutankhamen the great peoples that had built up civilization were losing their dominant position. Egypt's power was showing definite signs of weakness, which were intensified rather than caused solely by the pacifist policy of

Akhenaton and his sons-in-law. For even the vigorous rule of the powerful pharaohs of the nineteenth dynasty merely revived Egyptian power for a time before its final collapse. Fifty years before Tutankhamen, the Palace of Knossos had been destroyed in Crete, marking the downfall of the great pioneer of Mediterranean civilization to which Greece and Europe as a whole became heir. Babylonia also had reached the limits of her influence: and the weakening of these three earliest great powers allowed the Hittites and the Assyrians to struggle the one with the other for supremacy, crushing out such states as that of the Mitanni, and by exhausting themselves, so prepared the way for the eventual incursion of Persia into the Mediterranean area.

Another reason why the sudden weakening of Egyptian influence in Asia under Akhenaton and Tutankhamen is so important an event in the history of civilization is because it occurred at a time when the literature of the Jews was becoming crystallized in the shape that was destined to exert so tremendous an influence upon the history of belief and social practice. If Egyptian rule had not been weakened at this particular time and Palestine had not been subjected to the disturbing influences of Syrian, Hittite, and Assyrian interference, the Old Testament would not have been composed in the atmosphere of strife that gives it its distinctive tone and seems to us to-day unduly to exalt the importance of warfare and the value of military courage.

But if the weakness of Akhenaton and Tutankhamen contributed in some measure to the facilitation of strife in Palestine and its reaction upon the sacred literature of the world, the times in which these events occurred were pregnant with new trends in the development of civilization for which these weak kinglets could not be held responsible. Aryan-speaking people had recently made their appearance on the stage of history for the first time, in Asia Minor and around the head waters of the Euphrates in Syria, and in the approaching disruption of the powers of Western Asia, the influence of these people of Indo-

European speech was destined to make itself obtrusive in Persia and India and exert a growing influence upon religious beliefs and social practices.

But simultaneously with these events of far-reaching significance in Asia, the people of Europe also first intruded upon the attention of Egypt, and revealed the fact that a new orientation of political influence was in preparation.

Between Asia and Europe the disturbances in the Levant played some part in launching upon their world-wide career of exploitation the persistent trading people we know as Phœnicians, who were responsible for the rapid diffusion of the elements of civilization during several centuries from Tutankhamen's time onward. At the moment it is the fashion to scoff at the Phœnicians and their works: but no one who seriously studies the evidence relating to their achievements is likely to be deceived by this pose. For there is no doubt these people did fulfil the rôle attributed to them in the Book of Ezekiel.

The period which is so brilliantly illuminated by the discovery of Tutankhamen's tomb is thus perhaps the most critical period in the whole history of civilization. A new era was dawning and every scrap of information that sheds any light upon the circumstances of this fateful time is of tremendous interest to us in understanding the civilization under which we ourselves are living.

MAP OF THE ANCIENT EAST

20

CHAPTER II

EXPLORATION OF
THE THEBAN TOMBS OF THE KINGS

The work of modern exploration of the Valley of the Tombs of the Kings can be said to have begun in 1819 when the traveller Belzoni opened and wrote a description of the tomb of Seti I. In 1881 the discovery was made of a collection of royal mummies, many of which had been buried about thirty centuries ago in the Valley of the Tombs, and had been removed about 1000 b.c. and hidden in a chamber in the great cliff (behind Deir el Bahari) that faces the Nile across the Theban plain. This stimulated renewed interest in the famous necropolis, but it was not until 1898 that the work of exploration there was rewarded by the discovery of the tomb of Amenhotep II containing the mummy of that pharaoh himself—the only king's mummy ever found in his own tomb before the discovery of Tutankhamen's, in which it is confidently believed the mummy is present and undisturbed, an unprecedented circumstance which will make the investigations next winter peculiarly important. For the mummy of Amenhotep II had been badly plundered like all those discovered before or since until the opening of Tutankhamen's burial chamber made it practically certain that in it will be revealed for the first time to modern men the undisturbed tomb of an ancient Egyptian king.

When Mr Howard Carter was appointed Chief Inspector of Antiquities for Upper Egypt his chief function was to safeguard the antiquities in the Thebaid. The Egyptian Government through its Archæological Committee has been in the habit (until the present year, when the wise rule that encouraged serious archæological exploration is being revoked) of granting to archæologists whose competence was regarded as satisfactory permission to excavate on ancient sites, and the Antiquities Department allowed such workers to take out of the country half the antiquities brought to light. But the Valley of the Tombs of the Kings was excluded from the operation of this rule, because the Antiquities Department reserved for itself a site of such historical importance.

Hence when Mr Howard Carter took charge of the Theban inspectorate he was in a serious dilemma. The deserted Valley of the Tombs of the Kings, in the hidden depths of which was hoarded the remains of the vastest collection of valuable antiquities ever assembled, was in his charge, and alongside it the modern population of Luxor and Sheikh abd-el-Gournah, the most skilful and persistent group of tomb-robbers who had been habituated to the practice of this craft for many centuries. Yet he could not solve the difficulty by the most efficient form of control, that is, by carrying on excavations there, because the Antiquities Department had no funds for such work and, for the reasons already given, private excavators were not allowed to work in the Valley of the Tombs. Mr Carter was fortunate in being able to find a solution of the problem that evaded all these difficulties. Mr Theodore M. Davis, of Newport, Rhode Island, who was visiting Egypt as a tourist in the winter 1902-1903, was persuaded to place at the disposal of the Department of Antiquities the funds for exploration in the Valley of the Tombs without claiming any reward beyond the kudos which his action brought. Hence in 1903 Mr Howard Carter began excavating in the Valley at Mr Davis's expense and discovered the tomb of Thothmes IV. The mummy of this pharaoh, which had been found in 1898 by M. Loret in the tomb of Amenhotep II, was unwrapped after its original tomb was found; and at Mr Carter's suggestion, M. Maspero asked me to investigate it. Mr Davis published a magnificent volume giving a report of the work in the tomb and the results of the investigation of the mummy. In the following years the expedition financed by Mr Davis found six other important inscribed tombs, those of Queen Hatshepsut, Yuaa and Tuaa (the parents of Queen Tiy), King Siptah, Prince Mentuherkhepshef, King Akhenaton and King Horemheb, and nine uninscribed tombs, one of which contained the beautiful gold jewellery of Queen Tausret and of her second husband Seti II, and another the pieces of inscribed gold plate stolen during the reign of Horemheb from the tombs of Kings Tutankhamen and Ay.

FIG. 1.
Mummy of Thothmes IV.

Before the war Mr Davis had completed his share of the work. He imagined that he had found the tomb of Tutankhamen, and in the preface of the last of his series of magnificent reports he makes the remark: "I fear that the Valley of the Tombs is now exhausted." But it is a fortunate thing that Mr Howard Carter did not share this idea. After the war the late Lord Carnarvon, with whom Mr Howard Carter had been working since 1907, applied to the Antiquities Department, and was granted a concession to be allowed to continue in the Valley of the Tombs the work which the late Mr Theodore Davis had abandoned. The work carried out by Lord Carnarvon and Mr Howard Carter before they took over Mr Davis's concession led to some important discoveries, the chief results of which were published in 1912, in a magnificent volume *Five Years' Exploration at Thebes*.

In the Valley of the Tombs of the Kings they carried out real and thorough exploration, as no previous workers had done. Instead of making mere exploratory openings into the masses of rubble they began systematically to clear the ground, moving vast quantities of material—they are said to have moved as much as 200,000 tons—in the process. In spite of the discouragement of doing work of so exhaustive and expensive a kind with no further reward than a few unimportant pots, they pressed on, until on 5th November 1922 their indomitable persistence was rewarded with the most wonderful discovery ever made in the history of archæological investigation.

The day before he left London last January to return to Egypt Lord Carnarvon gave this account of the discovery. In the famous tomb of the Vizier Rekhmara no burial shaft could be found, and after searching for it near the tomb-building it was decided to try in the Valley of the Tombs. While cleaning the floor of the valley for this purpose, Mr Carter found a step cut in the rock and after further clearance he found a wall in the cement upon which was impressed the seal of the Royal Necropolis. Further examination revealed the presence of a tomb that had been entered soon after the burial. It bore the cartouche of the King Tutankhamen.

The story of the amazing treasures that have so far been discovered in the tomb has been told in the daily press day by day from November 1922 until April 1923, and Mr Harry Burton's photographs have given us a realistic idea of their appearance.

The plan of the tomb presents a marked contrast to the more familiar Theban burial places; but it becomes more intelligible when it is compared with those which were made at the heretic king's capital during the time of Akhenaton.

Of the four chambers in the tomb only one has up to now so far been examined, and when the inventory comes to be made of the annexe, which is now packed with furniture, and the room leading out of the burial chamber, the largest and most wonderful collection of ancient furniture that has ever been made will be revealed.

But the most marvellous revelations of all await the investigator next season when the shrines in the burial chamber are opened and the sarcophagus and the coffins within it are made to reveal to us how a royal mummy was prepared for its eternal home.

The plan of the tomb of Rameses IV, made more than two centuries later than the time of Tutankhamen, is the only evidence we have of the arrangement of the coffins within the shrines; but the coffins of Yuaa and Tuaa, the great-grandparents of Tutankhamen's wife, and especially the wonderful coffin made for Akhenaton, his father-in-law, have prepared us for what we are to find next winter. But the artistic inspiration revealed in the design of Tutankhamen's funerary furniture and the craftsmanship are so vastly superior to those displayed in other tombs that we cannot predict what gems of art will be found when the inner coffins are exposed.

Of the mummy itself we can predict the success of the embalmer's efforts, because the art of preserving the body was at its best in the period from Amenhotep II until Rameses II, but some very interesting points in the technique of embalming remain to be discovered. In the case of Amenhotep III, the latest mummy of the eighteenth dynasty so far examined, the new procedure for stuffing packing material under the skin was introduced for the first time. In the nineteenth and twentieth dynasties it was completely given up, only to be readopted in the twenty-first dynasty. It will be interesting to discover whether or not this procedure was still in vogue at the time of Tutankhamen.

The most interesting discovery of all that next season holds in store will be the equipment of jewellery with which the mummy will be provided. So far all that we know of such jewels has been derived from the recovery of odd fragments and the impressions left upon the mummy's wrappings by the pieces long since stolen.

FIG. 2.
Ancient Plan of the Tomb of Rameses IV with an
interpretation by Howard Carter and Alan Gardiner.

FIG. 3.

The Mummies of Yuaa and Tuaa, the latest complete mummies known before the time of Tutankhamen, and the mummy of Seti I, the earliest after him. These mummies will give some idea of the state of preservation likely to be revealed in Tutankhamen's mummy.

CHAPTER III

TUTANKHAMEN

During the course of the excavations in the Valley of the Tombs of the Kings made on behalf of the late Mr Theodore M. Davis in the years 1906 and 1907, a series of objects were discovered bearing the name of Tutankhamen. In all probability they were stolen from his tomb during the reign of Horemheb, only a few years after the pharaoh was buried.

Under a large rock, found tilted on one side near the foot of a high hill, the late Mr Edward Ayrton, who was in charge of Mr Davis's Exploration in 1906, found a beautiful blue glaze cup bearing the cartouche of Tutankhamen. In the following year, when the late Mr E. Harold Jones was superintending the work, a rock-cut chamber was found; and as it contained so many objects bearing the name of Tutankhamen it was assumed by Mr Davis that he had discovered that king's tomb. Hence the volume published in 1912 giving an account of the work of 1906, 1907, and 1908 (during the last of which the tomb of Horemheb was found on the south side of the chamber already mentioned) was entitled *The Tombs of Harmhabi* [Horemheb] *and Touatânkhamanou* [Tutankhamen] (Theodore M. Davis' Excavations: Bibân el Molük), and the late Sir Gaston Maspero gave accounts of all that was then known of the lives of both Horemheb and Tutankhamen. It is only right to add that Sir Gaston Maspero did not regard the chamber opened by Mr Harold Jones as the tomb of Tutankhamen. For in the closing paragraph of his report on the scanty information we have of Tutankhamen's life and achievements, he states: "I suppose his tomb was in the Western Valley, somewhere between or near Amenôthes III [Amenhotep III, the last royal mummy known to have been buried at Thebes before Tutankhamen, because Akhenaton and Smenkhara were buried at El Amarna, and removed to Thebes later] and Aiya [Ay, the successor of Tutankhamen]: when the reaction against Atonu and his followers was complete, his mummy and his furniture were taken to a hiding-place, as those of Tiyi and Khuniatonu had been, probably under Harmhabi, and there Davis found what remained of it after so many transfers and plunders. But this also is a mere hypothesis, the truth of which we have no means of proving or disproving as yet."

Although Sir Gaston was right in assuming that the chamber discovered in 1907 was not Tutankhamen's tomb, his hypothesis that the latter might have been in the neighbourhood of his predecessor (Amenhotep III) and his successor (Ay) has been shown by Mr Howard Carter's recent discovery not to be true. The chamber seems to have been nothing more than a safe (perhaps cut out by the workmen who were making a tomb for Horemheb) in which plunderers of the tombs of Tutankhamen and Ay hid their spoil. Why they were unable to rescue all the gold they stole and so hid away is not apparent. The chamber was buried at a depth of 25 feet and was almost filled with mud, which had been swept into it by the rain of many centuries. In this room was found a broken box containing several pieces of gold stamped with the names of Tutankhamen and his wife Ankhsenamen, and others bearing the name of his successor called the King's Father-in-law Ay and his wife Tiy, but without any title or prenomen. In the mud was found the very beautiful statuette made of fine translucent aragonite commonly called "alabaster." Apart from its value as a wonderful work of art this figure is interesting as the broad scarf around the loins is tied in the Syrian fashion. Unfortunately there is no inscription on it. M. Daressy makes the tentative suggestion that it may represent Ay before his succession to the throne.

When it is recalled that in the recently discovered tomb parts of the gold plating were found to have been torn off the throne and other pieces of furniture brought to light by Lord Carnarvon's expedition, it is interesting to note that the inscribed sheets of gold found in 1908 represent scenes of Tutankhamen's triumphs and captured prisoners such as would have adorned the tomb furniture that has been found mutilated. Other pieces of gold represent similar scenes from furniture plundered from the tomb of Tutankhamen's successor Ay.

A few days after the discovery of the chamber containing these stolen objects a pit was found, some distance away from it, in which there were large earthenware pots containing debris from a tomb, such as wreaths of leaves and flowers and small bags of powdered substance. The cover of one of these jars was broken and wrapped around it was a piece of linen bearing an inscription in ink which refers to the sixth year of Tutankhamen's reign.

In this volume, as I have already mentioned, the late Sir Gaston Maspero collected together the few scraps of information available in 1912 with reference to the life and reign of Tutankhamen.

In the British Museum there are two models of lions sculptured from red granite, one of which was made at the instigation of Amenhotep III for a temple in the Soudan. The other one may have been carved for Tutankhamen, who claims that he "repaired the monuments of his father Amenhotep." For nearly a century scholars have been discussing the question whether the use of the word "father" was intended to refer to his parentage, whether, in fact, Tutankhamen was a brother or half-brother of his father-in-law the heretic king Akhenaton, or whether the word was used simply as a term of respect for his predecessor. The problem still remains unsolved, for Tutankhamen's elevation to the throne was due to his marriage with the daughter of Akhenaton, the customary method in ancient Egypt for establishing a right to the kingship.

FIG. 4.

Tutankhamen receiving Ethiopian tribute from Huy.

At the time of his marriage and succession he belonged to the Aton faith, which his father-in-law had established, and his name was Tutankhaton. But as soon as Akhenaton died, Tutankhaton and his wife Ankhsenpaaton abandoned the heresy and returned to the orthodox faith of Amen. As a token of their conversion they changed their names to Tutankhamen and Ankhsenamen and left Akhenaton's capital for Thebes, the headquarters of the priesthood of Amen, who no doubt were responsible for Tutankhamen's sudden return to the old religion.

The little information we possess of his reign is derived mainly from the inscriptions upon the Theban temples restored by him after his return to the orthodox faith, though many of these records are palimpsests, for Horemheb replaced Tutankhamen's name on most of them. The two other chief sources of information are: (*a*) the piece of linen found in 1907, which is the only certain evidence that he reigned as long as six years; and (*b*) a remarkably interesting series of wall-pictures in the tombs of Huy at Kurnet (Murrai), which afford the only record we have of Tutankhamen's relations with Ethiopia and Asia. These pictures are among the most familiar records of ancient Egyptian life, having been used by Champollion, Lepsius, Brugsch and Piehl, and the inscriptions describing the scenes have been translated into English by Professor Breasted.[1]

FIG. 5.

Part of the Asiatic tribute presented to Tutankhamen by Huy.

---

1 *Ancient Records of Egypt*, Vol. II. pp. 420-427.

CHAPTER IV

THE SIGNIFICANCE OF THE DISCOVERY

When the eyes of all the world are focussed on the tomb of Tutankhamen and the fresh revelation it affords of the superb achievements of the ancient Egyptians in the arts and crafts, it is worth while to consider how this new discovery is likely to affect our attitude to the history of civilization and to promote a fuller recognition of the human motives that found expression in its creation and development. Apart from the demonstration it affords of the fabulous wealth that was hidden away more than thirty centuries ago in the Valley of the Tombs of the Kings, the new discovery appeals as an æsthetic revelation of dazzling brilliance rather than as an addition to our knowledge. So far its effect has been to force the scholar and the man in the street to take an interest in the civilization that was capable of producing such perfect works of art, and to ask themselves whether this precocious culture was really so exotic as it is commonly supposed to have been, or whether, on the contrary, such achievements on the very threshold of a yet unenlightened Europe did not exert a far greater influence than it is usual to accord them.

But at present we are concerned simply in considering what is the significance of the discoveries so far made; the furniture, which has never been surpassed in the perfection of its workmanship and exquisite decoration; linen of a fineness and a beauty of texture that have never been excelled; carved alabaster vases such as the world has never seen before; and statues that afford some justification for the ancient belief that they were, in truth, "living images." What is the meaning of all this lavish display of skill and beauty? Why was so much wealth poured into the hidden recesses of this desolate ravine, and the most exquisite products of the world's achievement in the arts and crafts buried out of sight in this strange necropolis? The true answers to these questions reveal the motive force that brought about the development of civilization and made Egypt the pioneer in its creation.

EMBALMING AND IMMORTALITY

All these elaborate preparations, the laborious and costly process of hewing the tomb out of the solid rock and furnishing it with such magnificence, were made because the ancient Egyptians believed that the king's body to be housed in it had been made imperishable. They imagined that when the body was embalmed the continuation of the king's existence had been assured. Hence they provided him with food and raiment, the furniture and amulets, the jewels and the unguents, and other luxuries which he had been accustomed to enjoy, before he was taken to his "eternal house" in the desolate Valley of the Tombs. There can be no doubt that in the early days of Egyptian history this naïve belief was regarded in all seriousness as the simple truth. In fact, the thoroughness with which at first the Egyptians gave concrete expression to their faith in making material provision for every want that the deceased might experience could only have been inspired by the confidence that all these preparations were indeed effective. This conviction was deeply rooted in the practice of mummifying the dead, preserving the body so that it should become incorruptible and everlasting; and this was supposed also to involve the feasibility of the prolongation of the dead man's existence.

The hope of survival was thus based upon the efficacy of the embalmer's art; and the extraordinary constancy with which for more than thirty centuries—for a span of years four times the length of time that separates us from the arrival of William the Conqueror in Britain—they persisted in their efforts to improve their methods and render more perfect this gruesome practice is a striking tribute to the fundamental importance of mummification to the Egyptians. The craft of the carpenter was first invented for the manufacture of coffins to protect the corpse; the stonemason's first experiments had for their aim the preparation of rock-cut chambers still further to ensure its safety; the first buildings worthy of being called architecture were intended to promote the welfare of the dead, to provide places to which relatives could bring food necessary for the dead man's sustenance, and a room to house his portrait statue—another art that was the outcome of the practice of mummification—which took his place at the temple of offerings and preserved his likeness for all time.

These elements of civilization, the arts of architecture and sculpture, and the crafts of the carpenter and the stonemason, were thus direct results of the custom of embalming. But its influence in moulding ritual and belief was no less profound and far-reaching.

EARLY BELIEFS

The belief in the possibility of the continuation of existence after death may have been (and probably was) much older than the Egyptians; but the evidence now available seems fairly decisive that the belief in immortality was not definitely formulated by mankind until the means had been devised of making the corpse everlasting, when "the corruptible body put on incorruption." Moreover, the ritual of the most primitive religions was based upon the practices of the early Egyptians for revivifying the mummy, or its surrogate, the mortuary statue, by burning incense, pouring out libations, opening its mouth to give it the breath of life, and performing a series of dramatic acts to animate it. By means of these ritual procedures it was supposed that the officiating priest was able to restore consciousness to the dead body and so make it possible for it not only to take an intelligent share in the life around it, but also to hear appeals for help and guidance and to answer such requests.

Egypt alone of the countries of antiquity provides the explanation of these strange beliefs and practices. They were devised by the concrete-minded people of the Nile Valley as part of a comprehensive philosophy of life and death which was formulated as a sort of life insurance, in accordance with the principles of which the deceased himself was supposed to be the beneficiary, and his reward an indefinite prolongation of existence.

This remarkable system of beliefs originated even before the beginning of civilization, sixty centuries ago; but the latter event was responsible for intensifying the conviction of its reality and increasing men's hope in its potency.

THE DAWN OF CIVILIZATION

Civilization began when the Egyptians first devised the methods of agriculture and invented a system of irrigation. The irrigation engineer was the first man in the history of the world to control and organize the co-operative work of his fellow-men, and become the ruler of a whole community. If there is one lesson more than another that history has demonstrated in Egypt, equally in ancient and in modern times, it is the absolute necessity of a strong and autocratic Government, because the conditions in the Nile Valley are such that the prosperity of the country and the welfare of the whole community is entirely dependent upon the just and equitable distribution of the waters of irrigation throughout the land. It is not to be wondered at that the engineer who successfully achieved this task, and in a very special and real sense controlled the lives and destinies of his people, became the king, whose beneficence was apotheosized after his death, so that he became the god Osiris, who was identified with the river, whose life-giving powers he controlled. For to a people who had never experienced anything of the kind before it must have seemed an altogether miraculous and superhuman act for one man to have in his absolute control the prosperity of a whole community and every individual unit of it.

The connection between this story and the tomb of Tutankhamen may not be apparent. But when it is realized that the original invention of the social system was so closely identified with the god Osiris, it will be understood that the ritual of mummification and burial aimed at identifying the deceased with Osiris, and by imitating the incidents of his story to secure for the deceased a fate like that of the god, whose life-giving powers were sought to grant the continuation of existence.

The early kings of Egypt, rich in their newly acquired control of the labour and wealth of their dominion, did not hesitate to squander both in the preparation of their tombs, in the vain belief that thereby they were making certain their own survival. Twenty centuries later, in the times of Tutankhamen, they were still obsessed with the same idea, and spent fabulous sums in preparing their tombs in the Biban el Moluk.

The peculiar importance of the study of these strange customs and beliefs in Egypt depends upon the fact that, not only were they invented by the Egyptians, and preserved in their entirety, so that the whole story of its development can be read in all their childish directness and simplicity, but also because other peoples of antiquity, to whose civilization Europe owes her own heritage, adopted some of the results of these Egyptian devices, and, after eliminating some of their cruder details, transformed them into the essentials of the world's civilization.

FIG. 6.
Part of a mace-head found by Mr J. E. Quibell at Hierakonpolis
in 1897-8, showing one of the earliest kings of Egypt engaged
in the task of cutting an irrigation canal.

Hence, in recovering the history of Egyptian cultural development, we are really probing into the sources of the customs and beliefs of our own everyday life and experience. Thus we must regard mummification as something more than an eccentric practice that excites our curiosity. For it played a fundamental part in shaping the development of civilization, both its arts and crafts, as well as its most vital customs and beliefs.

GIVING LIFE TO THE DEAD

If we turn to consider the process of mummification, and the aims of its practitioners, it will be found that throughout the long ages in which it was in vogue the Egyptian embalmer kept constantly striving to attain two aims. His first object was to preserve the actual tissues of the body as thoroughly as he could. But he was also attempting the much more difficult task of preserving the natural form of the body, and especially of the features. He was prompted to make this effort, not merely that the deceased should retain his distinctive traits in a recognizable form, but rather that the simulacrum should be the "living" image of himself. In other words, the aim was to make the representation of the dead man so life-like that he should, in fact, remain alive, and be certain of maintaining his existence. The early Egyptians seem to have entertained in all its childlike *naïveté* the belief that they were actually conferring vitality upon the image when they made it life-like. The Egyptian verb for describing the work of the sculptor who carved the portrait statue meant literally, according to Dr Alan Gardiner, "to give birth," in the sense of "giving life"; and there is no doubt they meant this idea of life-giving to be accepted as the simple expression of a fact, and not merely as a symbol or analogy.

It must not be forgotten that when these beliefs were first formulated, more than fifty centuries ago, there was no knowledge or understanding of the principles of physics and biology to hinder the adoption of such naïve fancies as the simple and obvious truth. There is no reason to doubt that the philosophers of those days did honestly believe in the possibility of prolonging existence by fulfilling all the conditions that seemed to them essential and adequate to the maintenance of vitality.

When mummification was first devised, probably at the time of the earliest dynasty (about 3400 b.c.) it was realized that if, in the climate of Egypt, the preservation of the tissues of the body was not very difficult to effect, the task of retaining the distinctive features was practically unattainable. All kinds of devices were tried, during the second, third, and fourth dynasties, by wrapping the mummy so as to simulate the human form, painting it, applying clay or resinous paste, and modelling it into a portrait statue upon the enshrouded mummy itself. When these devices failed to achieve the desired aim of making life-like portraits, the art of modelling statues of the deceased in stone or wood was invented, and paint and artificial eyes were used to make them as life-like as possible. The skill with which the Egyptians of the Pyramid Age overcame the technical difficulties of the sculptors' art and made life-size portraits which, as I have said before, could not untruthfully be called "living images," is one of the most amazing achievements in the history of art. But it was more than the triumph of a craftsman: it was the realization of a deeper desire to preserve the image, and so prolong the existence of the sculptor's model, the deceased, who was thus supposed to have been saved from annihilation.

In the first chapter of my book *The Evolution of the Dragon*, I have discussed this problem more fully.

FIG. 7.

Portrait of Hesi, circa 3000 b.c., to show the skill displayed even at the beginning of Egyptian history in carving portraits in wood. As a rule they were made in the round and life-size. This funerary portrait cut in low relief in wood is exceptional.

SUCCESS AFTER TWENTY CENTURIES

Although these early sculptors had achieved so signal a triumph, the embalmers never abandoned the hope of bringing their art to such a state of perfection as to make of the mummy itself the simulacrum of the deceased. With infinite patience and persistence they experimented through one millennium after another to attain this object. But it was not until the time of the twenty-first dynasty, more than twenty centuries after they first attempted to do it, that they were able to transform the mummy itself into a portrait statue. From the artistic point this represents to us a debasement of æsthetic motive and practice; but to the embalmer it was the culmination of his achievement. But it was also the prelude to the degradation of his art. For the technique became so complex and difficult of execution that failure became a common incident, and to disguise the evidence of such incompetence the practice grew up of paying chief attention to the external appearance of the wrappings rather than to the corpse.

But to us the complicated technique of the embalmers during the twenty-first dynasty appeals rather as ingenious trickery, a tampering with the natural body to give it a spurious and trumpery resemblance to a living being. Judged by our artistic standards there can be no doubt that the ancient Egyptian practice of mummification was seen at its best at the end of the eighteenth dynasty, that is about the time of Tutankhamen. The most successful results are revealed in the mummies of Yuaa and Tuaa and of Seti I (Fig. 3), which means that at the time when Tutankhamen was embalmed the craftsmen had the skill and the material resources to make as perfect a mummy as Egyptian ingenuity in the whole of its experience was capable of doing.

But the Egyptian tomb-robbers brought to the attention of the official world many mummies of the earlier part of the eighteenth dynasty, as well as some of those of the nineteenth and twentieth dynasties respectively before and after the culmination of the technical success in or about Tutankhamen's time which revealed only too clearly certain faults that it seemed desirable to remedy.

FIG. 8.
The "packed" mummy of a
Queen of the Twenty-first Dynasty.

The wholesale plundering of the Royal mummies in the twentieth dynasty, and the knowledge acquired by the priests when remedying the damage so inflicted, seem to have been responsible for the rapid transformation of the methods in the twenty-first dynasty. For this experience afforded them a unique opportunity of studying the results and appreciating the defects of their predecessors' work.

That they profited by this experience is evident from the changes they effected in their technique after they had realized wherein the methods employed during the twentieth dynasty failed to attain the desired aim. For their innovations were directed towards remedying the most obtrusive distortions found in the mummies of the nineteenth and twentieth dynasties. The sunken cheeks were filled out by means of packing them with linen or mud, artificial eyes were inserted, the nose, lips, and ears were protected from distortion by wax plates, and the cheeks were painted. Many other devices were introduced to convert the mummy from a shrunken caricature into a more life-like portrait.

Mummification reached its fullest and most successful development during the six centuries from 1500 b.c. to 940 b.c., which represents the period of the collection of royal mummies in the Cairo Museum. They reveal the ancient Egyptian practice of embalming in its highest perfection, and have provided most of the information we possess of the history of mummification.

I have called attention to the aims which the ancient Egyptians kept so persistently in view in constructing and furnishing the tombs of their kings. The pharaoh's body was embalmed to make sure of the continuation of his existence beyond the grave. The conviction that this object was really attained when the mummy was made and housed in an imperishable building induced them to furnish the tomb lavishly and to provide an ample store of food to sustain him and give him all the comforts and luxuries to which he was accustomed when he was living upon earth. But, to make doubly sure, they inscribed upon the walls of his tomb, upon his sarcophagus and coffins, and on papyri placed in the tombs, certain texts to make clear his identification with Osiris, with the practical object of ensuring that he should share the fate of the god and attain the immortality which the god had secured. Moreover, other devices were adopted to make the issue more certain.

Of the objects found in association with the mummies of Egyptian kings of the eighteenth dynasty to which definite cultural importance was attached, none is more remarkable than the so-called "germinating Osiris." Several examples of this singular symbol were found in the tombs of Tutankhamen's predecessors, as far back as Amenhotep II. (1420 b.c.), and as it was observed in its fullest development in the tomb of his successor, Horemheb (1315 b.c.), it is more probable than not that Tutankhamen's will also be similarly equipped. It consists of a shallow box about 5 ft. long, shaped so as to represent the god Osiris, wearing a crown and holding the crook and whip in his hands. By means of wooden partitions the features of the head, the necklace, the arms are represented. This shallow box was filled with earth in which barley was planted; when it germinated and the sprouts had attained two or three inches in height a closely-fitting lid was fastened on to the box by wooden pegs. The lid is slightly sculptured en ronde bosse, and painted yellow. The details of the body and the ornaments are indicated in relief, the effect of which is heightened by lines of black and red.

FIG. 9.
Drawing from Book of the Dead to illustrate the
Germinating Osiris, from Rosellini.

THE KING AND OSIRIS

The symbolism expressed in this remarkable procedure was in keeping with the motives which were explained earlier in this chapter, the identification of the dead king with Osiris (who was himself a dead king), whose magical powers as the bestower of renewed life and a continuation of existence after death was symbolized by the germinating barley.

But the procedure was richly charged with the deepest religious significance. I have already explained that the whole of the burial customs of the early Egyptians and the dramatic ritual which formed part of the tomb ceremonies were inspired by the desire to ensure the prolongation of existence. The body was made imperishable and protected by every means the relatives could devise: it was supplied with abundance of food and all the necessaries of life; and, above all, the "germinating Osiris" was there to complete the process and perpetually to animate and prolong the existence of the corpse. If its potency was derived from the reproduction of the form of Osiris, an equally vital part of its supposed magical power was due to the fact that it consisted of barley in the act of producing new life.

As the earliest cereal that was cultivated and the staple diet of the earliest civilized people—and the chief factor in creating their civilization—barley came to occupy a peculiarly distinctive rôle in early belief. It was the staff of life and the material from which beer was made, the drink which was regarded as "divine," in the sense that life-giving qualities were attributed to it, and to the ancient Egyptian the essence of divinity was the attainment of unlimited existence. But the form assumed by a grain of barley (*i.e.* its similarity to the organ of birth, the giver of life) led to the assimilation of its life-sustaining with definitely life-giving functions. It was identified with the Great Mother as a life-giver (in her forms as Hathor or Isis); and the "corn mother" acquired the reputation of being able to prolong existence in other ways than providing food and drink. The coffin texts of the Middle Kingdom (*circa* 2000 b.c.) translated by M. Lacau refer to the identification of the deceased with Osiris and barley, and in the Pyramid texts many centuries earlier the dead king is represented, as making the following claim: "I am Osiris. I live as the gods; I live as 'Grain'; I grow as 'Grain.' I am barley." (Professor Breasted's translation.) Just as the Nile (which was personified as Osiris) conveyed new life to the grains of barley by irrigating them, so the god was supposed to be able to grant a new lease of existence to the dead.

CHAPTER V

THE VALLEY OF THE TOMBS

It was about the year 1500 b.c. that the desolate and impressive ravine which is now known as the Valley of the Tombs of the Kings was chosen by King Thothmes I as the site for his tomb. His immediate predecessor Amenhotep I had observed the practice, which had prevailed since the temple was first invented, of building the tomb in association with it. For the temple was a development of the rooms provided at the tomb for the relations of the deceased to make offerings of food and drink to the dead for the essentially practical purpose of maintaining his existence. In these rooms also certain ceremonies were performed from time to time with the object of animating the dead man (or his portrait statue) so that he could enjoy the food and commune with his relations. But such functions were also part of the process of conveying "life" to him and so ensuring the maintenance of his existence.

In course of time as these ceremonies for conveying sustenance and life to a dead king assumed a wider significance the chamber of offering developed into a temple and a subtle change occurred in the meaning attached to the ritual. For instead of being regarded merely as a physical device for conveying food and the essence of life the ceremonies came to be regarded more and more as acts of worship of the dead king. When this happened the close nexus between the temple and the tomb was no longer so essential as it was in earlier times when the ceremonial in the former was intended to vitalize the corpse of the king (or his substitute the portrait statue). But it was not until the closing years of the sixteenth century b.c. (Thothmes I is believed to have died in 1501 b.c.) that the king began to prepare a tomb for himself miles away from his temple.

FIG. 10.
The end of the desolate Valley of the Tombs of the Kings at Thebes, the most impressive site in the whole of Egypt.

This geographical separation of the temple from the tomb had a far-reaching influence upon the functions of the former, and prepared the way for the modern conception of a house of worship, even though in Europe the ancient conception of the close association of a church and a churchyard (as a burying place) was retained. The practice inaugurated by Thothmes I of preparing royal tombs in the famous Theban Valley lasted from about 1500 b.c. until the end of the twentieth dynasty, about 1090 b.c.

Amenhotep III, who was buried in 1375 b.c., broke away from the observances of his four predecessors who were buried in the Eastern Valley and made his tomb in the Western Valley; and his famous son and successor, Amenhotep IV, the heretic king Akhenaton, made the more daring innovation of preparing a tomb at his new capital, the City of the Horizon of Aton, on the site of the modern Tell el Amarna. It was a rock-cut tomb in the mountains about seven miles to the east of his new capital— which Akhenaton built midway between Thebes and Memphis, the ancient capitals of Upper and Lower Egypt respectively. There he seems to have been buried in the red granite sarcophagus that is now broken into fragments; but his son-in-law Tutankhamen, when he reverted to the orthodox religion of Thebes, thought it proper to remove the mummy of his father-in-law from the City of the Horizon to the Theban necropolis and made for it the resting place in the Valley of the Tombs, which was discovered in 1907 by Mr Arthur Weigall, who as Inspector of Antiquities for Upper Egypt was supervising the excavations endowed by the late Mr Theodore M. Davis.

The fate of the mummy of Akhenaton's successor Smenkhara is unknown: but Tutankhamen came after him, and Mr Howard Carter's discovery has shown that he displayed his return to strict orthodoxy by making his tomb in the Eastern Valley among the worshippers of Amen. For some reason which has not been fully elucidated, his successor Ay made his tomb in the Western Valley and so was laid to rest alongside Amenhotep III, whose Minister he seems to have been during his life. He is supposed by some historians to have been the father or the foster-father of Nefertiti, the wife of Akhenaton.

FIG. 11.

An ancient Egyptian drawing (circa 1400 b.c.) illustrating
the arrangement of the tomb and temple about a millennium
earlier. The temple where the relations of the deceased made
offerings or animating ceremonies before the statue (or the
mummy itself) was then an essential part of the tomb, where
the actual body of the deceased was laid to rest.

Until the discovery of Tutankhamen's tomb in the Eastern
Valley last November it was believed (by Sir Gaston Maspero
and others) that it would be found in the Western Valley. Until
then Ay's was the earliest royal tomb, after that of Amenhotep
III, to be discovered, and as they were in the Western Valley, it
seemed probable that Ay's predecessor Tutankhamen had also
been buried there. But when making the secondary tomb for
Akhenaton in the Eastern Valley he seems to have made his own
tomb there also, and so resumed the old practice, which was

observed by all his successors for two and a half centuries with the exception only of his successor Ay.

This wonderfully impressive gorge (Fig. 10) is known to the modern Egyptians as the *Bab* (or *Biban*) *el Moluk*, the Gate (or Gates) of the Kings. It was known to travellers ever since it was made into the royal necropolis, and Greeks and Romans marvelled at the wonderful tunnel-like tombs there, as generations of tourists have done ever since. Strabo mentions his having seen forty of these tombs, but it is not clear from his account whether he did not include those of the Western Valley and perhaps the Tombs of the Queens and others.

FIG. 12

An old photograph of the great cliffs behind Deir el Bahari, showing this temple as it was in 1881 before it was excavated. The royal mummies were hidden in a cleft in these cliffs.

MAP OF THEBES

Modern research was inaugurated by the traveller Belzoni who opened the tomb of Seti I in 1819 and described the pictures on its walls (Fig. 20 is copied from his notebook) before they were damaged or destroyed. He brought to London the magnificent "alabaster" sarcophagus of this pharaoh, which is now in Sir John Soane's museum in Lincoln's Inn Fields. The year 1881 will always be memorable for the earliest discovery of Royal mummies. Five years later, when the wrappings were removed from such pharaohs as Seti I and Rameses II, modern men had the novel experience of gazing upon the actual faces of these famous rulers of the remotely distant past, whose exploits had resounded through the civilized world for thirty centuries and more. On several occasions in former years the discovery of Royal mummies had been reported; but in every case further investigation failed to justify such claims, for they proved to be merely intrusive burials of unknown people belonging to times much later than the rifled tombs in which they were found. Examples of such mistakes in identification are the eighteenth dynasty mummy, now in the Cairo Museum, which was found in a pyramid at Sakkara, and at one time was supposed to be the son of King Pepi, of the sixth dynasty; and the skeleton (not a mummy) in the British Museum from the pyramid of Mykerinus, which has repeatedly been referred to as the bones, or even as the mummy, of that pharaoh.

The discoveries made in the famous cache at Deir el Bahari in 1881, and in the Valley of the Tombs of the Kings during the decade 1898-1908, revealed the only actual mummies of members of the royal family so far recovered, although the skeletons of much earlier members of the ruling house were found by M. de Morgan in the pyramids of Dashur nearly thirty years ago.

Long before the recovery of the actual bodies of these famous rulers the statues and bas-reliefs of some of them had familiarized us with their appearance; and inscriptions on their monuments and the ancient writings of the Egyptians and their neighbours had made us acquainted with certain of their exploits. The plundered tombs of some of the great kings of the eighteenth and nineteenth dynasties have been known and visited by tourists from the times of the Greek domination of Egypt, and contemporary documents refer to others. Moreover, twenty years before the mummies themselves were revealed, the dealers in antiquities began to offer for sale a series of papyri (most of which came to this country) giving accounts of the desecration of the royal Theban tombs.

TOMB-ROBBERS' CONFESSIONS

In the late Lord Amherst's collection, which was recently sold in London, there was a judicial papyrus of the reign of Rameses IX (about 1125 b.c.), reporting the trial of eight "servants of the High Priest of Amen," who were arraigned for plundering the tomb of King Sebekemsaf of the thirteenth dynasty. The written depositions of the prisoners set before the pharaoh by the vizier, the lieutenant, the reporter, and the mayor of Thebes were translated by Professor Percy Newberry in these terms: "We opened the coffins and their wrappings, which were on them, and we found the noble mummy of the king. There were two swords and many amulets and necklaces of gold on his neck: his head was covered with gold. We tore off the gold that we found on the noble mummy of this god [*i.e.* the dead king who was identified with Osiris]. We found the royal wife also. We tore off all that we found from her mummy likewise, and we set fire to their wrappings. We took their furniture of gold, silver and copper vases, which we found with them." The prisoners who made this confession were found guilty, and sentenced "to be placed in the prison of the temple of Amen," to await "the punishment that our lord the pharaoh shall decide." There are several other famous papyri reporting trials of desecrators of the royal tombs. In the Abbott papyrus (in the British Museum) inspectors submit a report on the tombs that were said to have been plundered, but the only one that had actually been robbed was that referred to in the confession just quoted from the Amherst papyrus. The two Mayer papyri in the Liverpool Free Public Museums relate to plundering in the Valley of the Tombs of the Kings. One of these is of special interest at the present moment because it relates to the violation of the tomb of Rameses VI, which is immediately above that of Tutankhamen. The robbers were discovered as the result of quarrels among themselves about the division of the spoil. This was one of the most disgraceful incidents in the whole history of tomb-plundering. The robbers, in their haste to get at the gold and jewels upon the mummies, usually chopped through the bandages, and mutilated the mummy in the process. But when, in 1905, I removed the wrappings from the mummy of Rameses VI (which in ancient times had been removed to the tomb of Amenhotep II, where it was discovered by M. Loret in 1898), the body was found to be hacked to pieces. This was no mere accidental injury, but clearly intentional destruction of a malicious nature. It makes one realize the sort of vandalism Tutankhamen's tomb so narrowly escaped.

HIDING THE MUMMIES

The discovery of the royal mummies in 1881—and this applies with special force to the remains of the famous pharaohs Seti I and Rameses II—gave us the other side of the story, for it revealed the measures taken to protect the bodies of these kings from further injury, and the persistence with which the protectors of the tombs moved the mummies from one place to another in their endeavour to save them. The condition of affairs revealed in the tomb of Tutankhamen brings proof of what has long been suspected, that the work of the plunderer began soon after the closing of the chambers. But during the twentieth and twenty-first dynasties, when there was a rapid weakening of the Administration, tomb-robbing assumed proportions it had never attained before. The record inscribed upon the coffins of Seti I and Rameses II throws a lurid light on the extent of this loss of control. For a century and a half their mummies were moved from one hiding-place to another in the attempt to secure their safety. The mummy of the great Rameses was moved to the tomb of his father, Seti I, whose body for some time remained in its own alabaster sarcophagus, which is now in Sir John Soane's Museum in Lincoln's Inn Fields. But in the reign of Siamon (976-958 b.c.) the two mummies were hidden in the tomb of a queen called Inhapi, and about ten years later were moved again, this time to a tomb that had been originally prepared for Amenhotep I at Deir el Bahari. Here they, together with more than thirty other royal mummies, remained undisturbed for more than twenty-eight centuries, until about fifty years ago they were rediscovered, and the successors of the ancient tomb-robbers of Thebes once more resumed the old process of depredation. But the late Sir Gaston Maspero had not studied the papyri of the twentieth dynasty in vain, for he obtained a confession that is worthy of being set beside those recorded in the Amherst and Mayer papyri.

The story of the ill-treatment of the royal mummies and of their repeated removal from one hiding-place to another prepared us in some measure for the discoveries that were made when the shrouds and linen bandages were removed. But in spite of this the investigation was full of surprises. Several of the mummies after being hastily rewrapped (in the twentieth or twenty-first dynasty) were put into the wrong coffins. So that, for example, when the mummy supposed to be Rameses I (of the nineteenth dynasty) was unwrapped, an old white-haired lady was found embalmed in a way distinctive of the early part of the eighteenth dynasty. And again, when the mummy in the coffin of Setnakht (the first king of the twentieth dynasty) was examined, it was found to be that of a woman embalmed in the manner distinctive of the time of Setnakht's predecessor (Seti II, of the nineteenth dynasty); and it is probable that she is Queen Tausret, the wife in turn of the two kings, Siptah and Seti II. Such discoveries reveal the need for caution in claiming that the Valley of the Tombs of the Kings has yielded up all its hidden secrets. For there are many royal mummies that we know to have been buried there which have yet to be recovered.

FIG. 13.

The lid of the coffin that contained the rewrapped mummy of Amenhotep III, to show how it was labelled by the Priests of the twentieth dynasty and the record of an inspection written alongside it.

If the examination of the royal mummies reveals the thoroughness with which the tombs have been rifled—not one of the series has ever been found undisturbed—they also give us some idea of the value of the jewellery and amulets which excited the greed of the robbers thirty centuries ago. The torn and mutilated wrappings of the mummies often bear the impressions of magnificent pectoral ornaments, and of amulets on the forehead, neck, or limbs; and the occasional finding of fragments of these, made of gold, lapis lazuli, or carnelian, gives us some idea of the value and beauty of this extravagant equipment of the dead. But I have known only one instance of an object of any considerable intrinsic value escaping the diligent searching of these experienced robbers. During the examination (in 1909) of the badly plundered mummy of Queen Hontaui I found a large and beautifully embossed plate of pure gold, unique in size and in the elaboration of its design.

From these considerations we can safely predict that if, as seems now to be certain, the unplundered mummy is found in the tomb of Tutankhamen jewellery of great value and beauty of design will probably be found on it. The superb workmanship displayed in making these ornaments and amulets is known to us from the discoveries made by M. de Morgan in the Pyramids at Dashur in 1893. These gold pectoral ornaments inlaid with precious stones were wrought with an amazing perfection of technical skill many centuries before the time of Tutankhamen; but the jewellery of the eighteenth and nineteenth dynasties now exhibited in many museums (especially the Cairo Museum and the Louvre) reveals that the skill in making such works of art had not been lost. The quality of the workmanship revealed in the objects found in the first chamber of Tutankhamen's tomb should prepare us for the discovery on the mummy of ornaments even surpassing those of Rameses II in the Louvre (see Maspero, *Egyptian Art*).

But the chief interest in the discovery should be in the mummy itself, for the welfare of which all the elaborate arrangements were made. It is not merely because the mummies enable us to form some idea of the physical features of the kings and queens, and by appealing to our common humanity give their personalities a reality they would not otherwise possess;

nor is it because they often reveal evidence of age and infirmities; their chief interest is the light they throw on the history of the period and upon the development of the art of embalming.

Perhaps I can best make plain what is meant by this statement if I refer to specific illustrations of the former kind of contribution the study of mummies makes to the fuller understanding of history.

When in 1907 the bones were found that had once formed part of the mummy wrongly assumed to be the famous Queen Tiy, I discovered that they were the remains of a young man's skeleton, for which, if it had been normal, it was difficult to admit an age of more than twenty-six years, if indeed as much. Now the archæological evidence seems to leave no loophole of escape from the conclusion that these bones are actually the skeleton of King Akhenaton; but, on the other hand, the historical evidence seems to demand an age of at least thirty years (or, according to a recent memoir by Professor Kurt Sethe, thirty-six years) for the famous heretic pharaoh. This apparent conflict between the two classes of evidence has stimulated an intensive study of the historical data and of the medical history of Akhenaton himself; and the final outcome of the investigations is likely to provide a most illuminating revelation of the inner meaning of perhaps the most human and dramatic incident that has come to us from ancient times. The peculiar features of Akhenaton's head and face, the grotesque form assumed by his legs and body, no less than the eccentricities of his behaviour, and his pathetic failure as a statesman, will probably be shown to be due to his being the subject of a rare disorder, only recently recognized by physicians, who have given it the cumbrous name Dystocia adiposo-genitalis. One of the effects of this condition is to delay the process of the consolidation of the bones. Studying the history of modern instances of this affection the possibility suggests itself that Akhenaton might well have attained the age of thirty or even thirty-six years, although his bones are in a condition which in the normal individual is appropriate to the years twenty-two to twenty-six. It is tempting to speculate on the vast influence on the history of the world, not merely the political fate of Egypt and Syria in the fourteenth century b.c., but the religious conceptions of Palestine and the whole world for all time, for which the illness of this pacifist poet may have been largely responsible.

FIG. 14.

An inscribed stone from Tell el Amarna, showing Akhenaton, his queen Nefertiti, and their daughters, all represented by the sculptor as suffering from the same dystocia as Akhenaton himself.

There is still a vast amount of information to be got from the study of the royal mummies in the light of modern knowledge, and by the use of technical methods that are now for the first time available: and one of the hopes raised by the new discoveries is that it may be possible to set an example of how such work ought to be carried out, so as to extract from the remains of these ancient pharaohs all the information they can give us.

The importance of the study of the technique of mummification as a means of revealing the past history of civilization (by affording evidence of the diffusion of culture which was the chief factor in the process of cultural development) is too large a subject to embark on here. I mention it only because most of the exact information we have of the history of embalming has been derived from the royal mummies themselves.

In my pamphlet *The Migrations of Early Culture* (1915) I made use of the evidence afforded by the geographical distribution of the practice of mummification to demonstrate the diffusion to the ends of the earth in ancient times of elements of culture that were derived directly or indirectly from Egypt.

In the *Revue Neurologique* for 1920 two French physicians, Drs M. Ameline and P. Quercy, published a very curious memoir with the title "Le Pharaon Aménophis IV, sa mentalité. Fut-il atteint de Lipodystrophie Progressive?" I have used the adjective curious with reference to their work, because they have put forward a carefully reasoned statement in support of the diagnosis they suggest, but do not seem to have made any attempt to make themselves acquainted with the evidence provided by the remains of the pharaoh. When it is recalled that in 1912 I gave a detailed account (*The Royal Mummies*, Catalogue Générale du Musée du Caire) of the broken bones which were all that was left of the mummy of the pharaoh (no trace of the mummy of his mother, Queen Tiy, has been found), it is surprising to find in a scientific journal the following statements, written ten years after the appearance of my official report was published:—"on a retrouvé récemment (1905), à Thèbes même, les *momies* du pharaon *et de sa mère Tii*," and, referring to the remains of Akhenaton, *i.e.* the broken fragments of the skeleton, "La momie, recouverte de feuilles d'or délicatement repoussé

63

et d'un réseau d'or avec pierres et verres colorés, *est également exceptionnellement belle, mais ces ornements empêchent naturellement d'examiner le corps du pharaon aux rayons X et, a fortiori, d'en practiquer l'autopsie?*" (*op. cit.*, p. 451. All the italics are mine).

I have quoted these purely imaginary statements to emphasize the fact that the distinguished physicians who made them were totally ignorant of the conditions revealed in the skull, and based their diagnosis wholly upon the pictures of Akhenaton and the history of his achievements. They describe the condition of progressive lipodystrophy as an affection characterized on the one hand by a progressive and complete disappearance of the subcutaneous fat of the upper part of the body; and, on the other, by a marked increase of the adipose tissue below the loins. The first example of this strange affection was described by Barraquer in 1907, but it is exceedingly rare in adult men. In fact the authors remark that "it would indeed be curious if a pharaoh, dead for thirty-five centuries, should provide a second case (after Gertsmann's) of the occurrence of this condition in an adult man."

It is unfortunate that these physicians neglected to study the report which I wrote for the General Catalogue of the Cairo Museum, published in the volume *The Royal Mummies* in 1912. For they would then have realized that the slight hydrocephalus, the indication of an early overgrowth of the jaw such as occurs in acromegaly, and then the gradual assumption of a feminine contour of figure, with a delayed union of the epiphyses, suggest the possibility that Akhenaton may have been the subject of Dystocia adiposo-genitalis.

The form of the head in Akhenaton, his daughters and some of the members of his family, more than half a century before his time, raises a problem of great difficulty and complexity.

FIG. 15.
A painted wooden portrait
bust of Nefertiti, wife of Akhenaton.

FIG. 16.
The skull of Akhenaton seen from the left side.

There is no doubt that the slight malformation of Akhenaton's head was due to pathological causes. It is equally certain that the gross distortion of the heads of his daughters, represented in the statues from Tell el Amarna which are now in Berlin, are the result of artificial deformation such as was and still is practised upon young children in Asia Minor and Northern Syria, with the royal family of which Akhenaton's family was linked by close ties. But in addition the mummy of a boy in the tomb of Amenhotep II, which was certainly embalmed in the reign of that pharaoh and is probably the body of his son, has a skull which is exceptionally broad and flat, and when viewed from the front presents an appearance curiously similar to the portrait statues of Akhenaton's daughters. The full significance of these peculiarities cannot be interpreted until the royal mummies now in the Cairo Museum are submitted to a thorough re-examination.

CHAPTER VI

THE STORY OF THE FLOOD

Just half a century ago[2] the proprietors of *The Daily Telegraph* arranged with the Trustees of the British Museum to send Mr George Smith to Mesopotamia to search in the ruins of the library of Ashur-bani-pal at Nineveh for missing fragments of inscribed tablets to fill the gaps in the *Chaldean Account of the Deluge*. The announcement of the discovery (in December 1872) aroused an intense and world-wide interest, and *The Daily Telegraph* provided the funds for the new expedition. Although this version of the Story of the Flood was discovered in an Assyrian library no older than the seventh century b.c., Mr George Smith predicted that the future would reveal it to be the survival of a more ancient version that had also indirectly been the inspiration of that recorded in the Book of Genesis. The recent discovery of the Sumerian prototype of this story, which was put into writing more than twenty centuries before the record in Ashur-bani-pal's library, is a remarkable confirmation of George Smith's prediction.

It will come as a surprise to most people to learn that the Valley of the Tombs in Egypt has provided the information which is destined in time to afford the explanation of the early history of the Story of the Flood, before it began to exert a strange fascination upon the minds of men that led to its diffusion throughout the world.

Inscribed upon the walls of the tomb of Seti I in the

---

2   This was written in January 1923.

68

Theban necropolis—less than seventy years after the burial of Tutankhamen—is the remarkable story of the Destruction of Mankind. In spite of the fact that it was inscribed in this tomb as recently—in comparison with the Sumerian story—as 1300 b.c., the strange confusion of archaic references which has made it so unintelligible to most modern scholars reveals the fact that its origin must be referred back to the fourth millennium. Although in the narrative found in Seti's tomb the destruction is not brought about by the Flood, it is clear that the Egyptian and the Mesopotamian stories have a common origin and a common motive. For the essential incident in the latter is not the Flood, but the Destruction of Mankind which it brought to pass.

If it be asked why this venerable story should be inscribed in the tomb of an Egyptian pharaoh, the answer is that its aim was to secure for the dead king those boons the attainment of which was the central motive of the tale. It records how old age began to affect the king, upon whose strength and virility the welfare of the whole community depended (see Chapter IV), and he became very sorely troubled when his subjects began to murmur about the failure of his powers, because in olden days the only way of safeguarding the prosperity of the kingdom, which was supposed to be wholly dependent upon the strength of its ruler, was to slay him when he began to fail and put in his place one whose vigour was at its prime.

The essence of the story, which made it potent as a charm to secure the continued existence of the king (and it was for this reason that it was inscribed upon the walls of the king's tomb) was that it describes how the ageing king circumvented fate (and the conventions of archaic society) by rejuvenating himself. The elixir of life was the blood of his slaughtered subjects; and the crime that was charged against them—the impiety and disloyalty, the original sin—was that they were murmuring among themselves about the king's failing health. But when they had been slaughtered and the king had attained a renewal of his youth, he was overcome by the boredom of too

69

prolonged an existence upon earth. So he mounted upon the back of the Celestial Cow and thus reached heaven and attained immortality.

This remarkable story, which was intended as a magical device for securing the same fate for the pharaoh of the fourteenth century b.c. as his remote prototype is said to have attained, also contains the germs of most of the mythology that has lasted longest and spread most widely in the early history of civilization. Although, so far as we are aware, this story is not found in Tutankhamen's tomb, there is no doubt that it was current at his time, because it was inscribed upon the walls of one of his successor's tombs little more than half a century later, and the narrative is obviously very old, being packed with archaic allusions and forms of expression. I have referred to it here because the symbolism expressed in some of the funerary furniture in Tutankhamen's tomb is explained by this mythical story recorded in those of Seti I and Rameses III. The question of interpretation I have discussed in another chapter, dealing with the funerary couches, and I have mentioned the Destruction of Mankind to call attention to the dominant motive—the Giving of Life and the Attainment of Immortality—which inspires every feature of the funerary ritual with tiresome persistence. For in the myth mankind was destroyed to provide the elixir of life for the king so that he might attain to the immortality, which was the distinctive prerogative of a god. The blood of the slaughtered saints was the elixir by which the mortal dweller on earth put on the immortality of a celestial being. The motive assigned in the story for destroying mankind was their sinfulness or disloyalty, which was more exactly defined by accusing them of spreading rumours of the king's increasing age and weakness, a form of report to which the ruler was peculiarly sensitive, because the admission that his strength and virility were failing was tantamount to a capital sentence. In the remotely distant age, from which the germs of this story came down to the time of Seti I, the ageing king had to be killed to make way for a more youthful and vigorous ruler. Hence one cannot marvel at the king's sensitiveness when his people murmured about his failing powers.

I have already referred to the fact that this accusation of disloyalty was the earliest version of what theologians call "original sin," and the story itself the prototype of that which under a modified form appears in the Book of Genesis. The primitive account of the slaying of mankind became confused with the inundation of the Nile, and the blood of the slaughtered human race and the blood-red inundation of the river became identified the one with the other. Though originally both events were regarded as beneficent and identical in their results, that is renewing the king's strength and the country's prosperity, when the story spread abroad to foreign countries a certain element of confusion crept into the narrative, and the destruction of mankind was attributed to the Flood. But it found a place in religious literature, not because it exemplified the wrath of the gods against sinful man, but because it explained how the king rejuvenated himself and attained the status of a god. The evidence provided by these Egyptian tombs gives us an insight into the motives underlying the religious beliefs of every people who came into relationship, directly or indirectly, with the arbitrary system of explaining the means of attaining immortality devised by the ancient priesthood of Egypt. It illustrates one of the ways in which these investigations in Egypt can illuminate ancient Jewish literature.

One of the peculiarities of Egyptian customs and beliefs is due to the fact that what the concrete-minded Egyptian naïvely did and said is to be interpreted in the literal and obvious sense that he attached to these acts. Among no other people can we similarly detect all the stages in the logical development of the practices and beliefs of civilization—and not only are the various stages preserved in Egypt, but in so crudely childlike a guise that he who overcomes the impulse to seek for some recondite or cryptic meaning in things which are really simple can read their plain story as their inventors intended it.

It is this fundamental fact that gives the study of Egyptian customs and beliefs its tremendous importance. The essential elements of civilization were originally invented by the Egyptians, who gave them simpler and more obvious expression than other peoples, who borrowed them ready-made without acquiring the connecting stages in their development or the naïve explanation of their meaning.

I have introduced this subject for consideration as an introduction to the study of the funerary equipment of Tutankhamen's tomb, to which the next chapter will be devoted.

CHAPTER VII

GETTING TO HEAVEN

It is not my intention to attempt to discuss the equipment of Tutankhamen's tomb. Readers of the daily papers and the illustrated weeklies will already be aware of the vast quantity of furniture and of the fact that even those who were already familiar with the superb design and workmanship displayed in the objects from such tombs as those of Thothmes IV, Yuaa and Tuaa, and Akhenaton were amazed at the new revelation of Egyptian craftsmanship revealed in scores of the things found in Tutankhamen's tomb, the throne, a superb work of art, the no less wonderful chariots, chairs, couches, statues, sandals, textiles and jewellery, and above all the impressive canopy or shrine. Archæologists familiar with all the marvels of Egyptian art, now treasured in the museums scattered throughout the world, have exhausted their vocabularies of wonder and admiration in attempting to depict the splendours of Tutankhamen's tomb. The outstanding feature of the discovery is, in fact, the recovery of so vast a collection of superb works of art and the new revelation it affords of the dazzling brilliance of Egyptian civilization thirty centuries ago.

But in this book I am concerned more especially with the cultural significance of the funerary equipment.

In the first place the objects found in the tomb belong to two distinct categories, those which were used by the deceased when alive, and others specially made for funerary purposes. This distinction seems to be brought out most clearly in the comparison of the chariots in the vestibule and in the burial chamber respectively.

I do not propose to enter into any further discussion of the contents of the wonderful shrine or canopy which is to be investigated next winter, nor to attempt to anticipate the result of the examination of the so-called "canopic" chest, which is said to be a unique example of the sculptor's art. The experience gained in investigating the contents of such chests in other tombs gives one confidence in assuming that the heart of Tutankhamen will not be found in it, as so many writers imagine, but that its four compartments will contain respectively the liver, lungs, stomach and intestines of Tutankhamen, his "heart and reins" being left in his body.

From the cultural point of view the most interesting articles of furniture found in Tutankhamen's tomb are the three lofty couches fashioned in grotesque shapes to represent conventionalized animals, cow, lion, and hippopotamus respectively. Although such couches are thoroughly Egyptian in design and are familiar in pictures from Egypt and the Soudan, they have never been seen before. They are worth discussing in some detail, because they express the concreteness and naïvety of Egyptian belief mentioned in the last chapter in a way that brings home to us the essential distinction of the religion of the ancient dwellers in the Nile Valley.

The problem of getting to heaven after death was approached by the Egyptian theologian as though it were essentially a physical proposition. How was the dweller upon earth to reach the world in the sky? What vehicle could he employ to reach the celestial realms? Speaking recently of Christian Englishmen in the twentieth century, Dean Inge is reported to have said that "a topographical heaven, so impossible scientifically, was so difficult to dispense with as an aid to the imagination." But to the ancient Egyptian belief in such a topographical heaven was a cardinal article of faith, and the geography of the Elysian fields and the details of the path leading to it were mapped out with all the meticulous precision of a modern guide-book. The dead man was often provided with a chart to find his way along the path that teemed with difficulties and dangers.

But although there were scores of different devices for securing a safe transit to the celestial regions, there was one vehicle which from the very beginning of Egyptian history enjoyed a special reputation as the appropriate means of protecting the dead and conferring life and immortality upon him by conveying him to the other world. The Celestial Cow Hathor not only conferred life upon mortals by giving them birth: she also sustained them throughout life by giving them the divine milk, and at death she conveyed them to the sky.

In the famous inscription upon the walls of the tomb of Seti I, to certain passages of which I referred in the last chapter, there is a remarkable story of the function of the Divine Cow Hathor or Nut as a means of raising the dead king to the sky to reach the home of the gods. After being rejuvenated by the goddess the king became oppressed with the boredom of life upon earth amongst his tiresome subjects, who had shown their disloyalty to him by referring to his old age and failing powers. So he decided to leave the earth and proceed to the sky. Hence he mounted upon the back of the cow and got to heaven, where he assumed his godhead by becoming identified with the sun.

This function of the cow in acting as a vehicle to convey the mummy to its celestial home is one which was repeatedly depicted in the ancient Egyptian monuments. But the cow's solicitude for the welfare of the dead was frequently shown in other ways. A favourite *motif* for the Egyptian sculptor was the representation of the Divine Cow, Hathor, protecting the dead king or permitting him to obtain an elixir of life by drinking milk from her udder. In his book *Egyptian Art* (1913) the late Sir Gaston Maspero devotes to this subject a whole chapter (XI) illustrated with six beautiful photographic plates of such cow-statues ranging from the time of Amenhotep II (1440 b.c.) to more than a thousand years later. But we know that the protective function of the Cow Hathor was portrayed in other ways as early as the time of the Pyramid-builders (for example, the beautiful slate statuettes found by Professor Reisner in the Pyramid Temple of Mykerinus of the fourth dynasty, about 2800 b.c.), and the still earlier representation of her upon the slate palette of King Narmer of the first dynasty, about 3400 b.c. For several reasons this palette is a historical document of unique importance. Engraved upon it is the earliest example of writing that has come down from antiquity: but it is of interest in connexion with the discussion in this chapter. For at the upper corners of the palette the cow-headed Hathor is depicted and as a further protection the king wears upon his belt four cows' heads (Fig. 18) in place of the cowrie amulets of more primitive peoples.

FIG. 17.
Cow carrying a dead man to heaven.

The Celestial Cow, Hathor, was a divinity of the dead, for she was the Giver of Life who was supposed to be able to prolong existence beyond the grave, and as she was also identified with the sky she became the appropriate vehicle to convey the dead to the celestial regions where the sun-god dwelt.

FIG. 18.

Narmer's belt with four Hathor cows' heads, circa 3400 b.c.

The most bizarre objects found in the vestibule of Tutankhamen's tomb are the three ceremonial couches, one representing the Celestial Cow, Hathor, the second the same goddess in her lioness form, or more probably her son and representative Horus in the form of a lion, and the third Tauert, the hippopotamus goddess, who was the divine midwife.

In the numerous accounts of these remarkable monstrosities that have appeared, I have not seen any attempt to explain their significance. Although such grotesque examples of mortuary furniture have never been seen before, the bas-reliefs upon the walls of tombs in Egypt and Ethiopia, and the pictures illustrating the Book of the Dead inscribed on papyri, have made us familiar with them. Moreover, the chapters of the Book of the Dead relating to "the raising of the funeral bed" leave no doubt as to the ritual significance of these couches.

The sides of the Hathor couch are grotesque models of the Divine Cow, the earliest of the Great Mothers who were believed to have bestowed life and prosperity on mankind. It may seem strange that the artists of Tutankhamen's time should have perpetrated such a monstrosity as this Hathor couch. When religious motives impelled the designers to fashion a piece of furniture in imitation of so uncouchlike a creature as a cow, the artist was set a task which was almost impossible of realization unless he sacrificed his artistic ideals. There can be no doubt that in this case he escaped the dilemma by repressing his æsthetic feelings and abandoning himself whole-heartedly to the task of devising a model which was almost wholly religious in conception.

To understand why the cow, of all creatures, should have been selected for this purpose, we must remember the relentless logic and persistency that inspired all the preparations of the tomb and its furniture. The mummification of the body and the elaborate arrangements for protecting it and ministering to its wants were due to the belief that the continuance of the deceased's existence had been secured by these preparations. But to make doubly certain, no device that would contribute to the attainment of this aim was neglected. Inscriptions were made on the walls of the tomb, on the sarcophagus and coffins, and on papyri to ensure the identification of the deceased king with Osiris, so that he might be made to share the god's fate. A figure of Osiris was made, as I have explained elsewhere, out of the sacred barley, every grain of which was regarded as a model of the life-giving Great Mother, and as such a supply of vital essence to maintain the deceased's existence. From time to time dramatic ceremonies were held at the tomb (or in the temple associated with it in far-off Thebes) to reanimate the dead and help him to persist.

FIG. 19.
Pictures of three couches represented on the
walls of the tomb of Seti I, from Belzoni's sketches.

For, once the ancient Egyptians had persuaded themselves that they could work out their own salvation, and that the kingdom of heaven could be attained by certain physical and magical procedures, they spared no pains to pursue this train of thought and action with tiresome persistence to the most surprising ends.

The Great Mother was originally nothing more than the personification of an amulet, like a cowrie shell or a grain of barley, that was supposed to be able to exert the essentially maternal function of life-giving. Then, when cattle were domesticated and mankind discovered for the first time that cow's milk could be used for feeding human children, people were profoundly impressed with this revelation of the cow's kinship with the human family. They regarded her as the foster-mother, and then as the actual mother of mankind, and identified her with the Great Mother Hathor, whose earliest form was (even sixty centuries ago) that of a Divine Cow. But if the Great Mother was at one and the same time a cowrie, a grain of barley, and a cow, she was also identified with the moon, which in a very special sense was supposed to control the life-giving powers of womenkind.

Hence the belief developed that if the Great Giver of Life and Immortality was both a cow and the moon, she was the appropriate vehicle to convey the dead king to the celestial realms in the sky. And so, as the nursery rhyme puts it, "the cow jumped over the moon." That the cow represented in the couch is a symbol of the sky is shown by the stars on the under surface of the body. The height of the couches also was an additional indication of their identification with the sky. In all periods of Egyptian history painters and writers were fond of depicting this episode of the conveyance of the dead king to heaven on the cow's back. This incident is shown and explained in the inscriptions on the walls of Seti I's tomb, to which I have already referred. But in later times it became common to represent the Divine Cow (or its lioness surrogate) conveying the dead man or his actual mummy to the sky, and in pictures of funerals to find the mummy borne on just such couches as have actually been found in the tomb of Tutankhamen. The object of the cow-shaped couch was to ensure by magical means this translation of the deceased to heaven. The story of the Destruction of Mankind gives the Egyptian's own interpretation of the incident. The influence of this Egyptian conception of animal "vehicles" for gods spread far and wide throughout the world in ancient times, for if such a creature could convey the dead king to the celestial regions and confer upon him the means of attaining immortality, which was the distinctive attribute of divinity, such an animal vehicle was an appropriate symbol and pictorial determinative of a god. The identification of the Great Mother with the cow was the beginning of the social system known as totemism.

The explanation of the lioness form of the Great Mother is also given in the inscription in Seti I's tomb. When the goddess was called upon to rejuvenate the ageing king, the only elixir of life known in her pharmacopœia was human blood. Hence, she was driven to the necessity of slaying a human being, and her murderous action was compared to that of a man-slaying lioness, with which she was identified. But as the lioness was a particularly appropriate form to symbolize the Great Mother's ability to protect the mummy from the perils that lurked in the pathway to the other world, it became an even more favourite form of the funerary vehicle than the gentle cow. At any rate, in the pictures of funerary couches the lioness form is much commoner than the cow-form. The same grotesque form of the lion has survived in modern heraldry.

But other ideas found expression in the lion-symbolism. For example, on some of the beautiful pieces of furniture found in Tutankhamen's tomb the king himself is represented as a human-headed lion trampling on his foes, and many of his predecessors before him, Thothmes IV for example, were similarly represented. Even as far back as the time of the Pyramids was not Mykerinus (2800 b.c.) represented as a human-headed lion in the gigantic Sphinx at the Giza Pyramids?

This representation of the king as a lion, which typifies his identification with Horus, is inspired by another chain of ideas. Although at the time of Tutankhamen, and in fact throughout the whole history of Egypt in dynastic times the sun-god was dominant in Egypt and Horus himself was a sun-god, the rôle that he took as the guardian of the dead was inspired by the more ancient Osirian faith. It was the living king Horus who was responsible for tending the dead king Osiris; and it was believed that the continued existence of the god (the dead king Osiris) was wholly dependent upon the services rendered by Horus. Thus it was Horus who performed the divine function of conferring immortality upon Osiris, and also upon the dead king Tutankhamen, who was identified with Osiris. Presumably the act of being borne upon the lion-couch was symbolically equivalent to being put into the care of Horus, not the Horus represented upon the furniture in the tomb, the lion-avatar of Tutankhamen who tramples his enemies under foot, but the son of Osiris, who holds out the promise of conferring upon the dead king the boons that he is credited with having given to Osiris— eternal life and protection. The confusion between these two aspects of Horus is brought out very clearly in a very interesting picture recently discovered by Professor George A. Reisner (and reproduced in *The Illustrated London News*, 10th February 1923, p. 204), engraven upon a monument in the Soudan several centuries later than the time of Tutankhamen. The lion-couch is represented supporting the mummy of King Ergamenes, whose head is portrayed in the form of the falcon of Horus. Above the mummy is the star-spangled sky, below which is seen the sun's disc emitting five streams of life-giving emanations to the dead king. In the Book of the Dead Chapter LXXVIII is called that "whereby one assumeth the form of the Sacred Falcon" and the deceased is represented as saying "I display myself as the Sacred Falcon whom Horus hath invested with his soul for taking possession of his inheritance from Osiris" (Renouf). The possibility suggests itself whether the lion-couch was intended to symbolize, as the cow-couch unquestionably was, the transference of the dead king to the sky to be united with the sun and identified with the solar deity Re. If so, perhaps the five streams of V-shaped emanations pointing to the disc were meant to represent the sun drawing the mummy, the dead Horus, to the sky.

In his monograph of the *Tomb of Amenemhēt* Dr Alan Gardiner reproduces a text (Plate XXX A) including a pictorial arrangement of hieroglyphs in the form of stars above the mummy borne on the lion-couch, which he translates as a statement that the dead man "wishes to be placed among the stars in the firmament" (p. 119).

The same design occurs in the pictures illustrating the Book of the Dead. The funerary couch is usually represented in the lion-form, the cow- and hippopotamus-varieties being much less frequently adopted.

In the pictures of funerals it is not uncommon to see the mummy borne upon a lion-shaped couch placed within the funerary canopy or shrine (as in the first of the pictures from the Book of the Dead, Fig. 20). Good examples are given by Dr Alan Gardiner and Mrs de Garis Davies in *The Tomb of Amenemhēt* (1915), Plates XII and XXIV, of the reign of Thothmes III, a century before Tutankhamen. No doubt this is due partly to the significance attached to the conception of Horus as the guardian of Osiris, but also possibly to the idea that Horus fought the enemies of Re and was the best protector of the deified dead.

FIG. 20.

Three vignettes from different papyri of the Book of the Dead,
representing the lion-couch bearing the mummy within its
canopy, a mummy lying on its funerary couch with three solar
emanations coming down from the sky, and a third where the
bird-soul is bringing to the mummy the symbol of eternity.

But underlying the whole of the lion-symbolism are two fundamental ideas which gave meaning to it. In the very ancient story of the Destruction of Mankind, which in a relatively modern and much distorted form was inscribed upon the walls of the tombs of several of Tutankhamen's successors, the goddess Hathor (the Divine Cow) is reported to have made a human sacrifice in order to obtain the blood wherewith to rejuvenate the senile king (in the story Re, the king upon earth who had not yet been elevated on the cow's back to the sky to become the sun-god). Hence she acquired the reputation as a slayer of men and was identified with a lioness, and called Sekhmet, the Destroyer. Thus the lioness and the cow were both forms assumed by the Great Mother Hathor. But in the development of the myth of the Destruction of Mankind the god Horus takes the place of his mother Hathor, and the bull and the lion take the place formerly occupied by the cow and the lioness. In the case of the funerary couches the Cow of Hathor is found alongside the lion of Horus, but occasionally one finds in late tombs the mummy represented as being conveyed to the celestial realms by a bull instead of the more usual cow. A good example of this is to be seen in the Museum of the Society of Antiquaries in Edinburgh.

The third couch is modelled in the form of a grotesque caricature of a hippopotamus, Tauert, another representative of the Great Mother Hathor. But her special duty was to act as a midwife at the births of gods and kings. In pictures she is often associated with the Hathor Cow at the door of the tomb in the Mountain of the West; and presumably her function was to preside at the rebirth of the dead king by which a new lease of life beyond the grave was conferred upon him.

If it seems far-fetched to regard the hippopotamus couch as symbolizing rebirth, it should not be overlooked that in the so-called "Birth Terrace" of the temple at Deir el Bahari[3] lion-

---

3 See Egypt Exploration Fund publication, *Deir el Bahari*,
  II, Plate LI.

headed couches are represented in the birth scene of Queen Hatshepsut. As I have pointed out already all three animals, cow, lioness, and female hippopotamus, represent primarily different forms of the same goddess Hathor.

FIG. 21.

Scene from The Book of the Dead (Papyrus of Ani) in which the three givers of divinity are seen, the cow at the entrance to the tomb, the hippopotamus with her, and Horus on guard.

The Egyptian custom of making these grotesque animal-shaped couches to symbolize the transference of the dead to the celestial regions and the conferring of immortality and deification upon them exerted far-reaching and manifold effects as it was diffused abroad among other peoples. I shall mention three examples of these diverse influences. The belief implied in such symbolism that a king borne by such an animal vehicle was transformed into a god led to the use of such designs in the representations of gods. Hence it became common in Syria and Mesopotamia, in Greece and India, and far away in outlying parts of the world where the influence of these civilizations played some part, directly or indirectly, to find gods and goddesses represented on animal vehicles, such as the bull or cow, the lion or lioness, or some fantastic composite monster, dragon or makara. The whole conception of animal vehicles, which plays such a large part in the religious symbolism of India, Eastern Asia and Central America, is a purely Egyptian fancy that finds such grotesque expression in Tutankhamen's funerary couches, no less than in the borrowed symbolism that was spread abroad from Egypt to Asia and America.

FIG. 22.

The goddess Astarte borne on her lioness, symbolizing the attainment of immortality, which was the distinctive attribute of a deity.

Another expression of the essential meaning of these couches was the belief that the placing of the corpse or mummy on a raised stage was magically efficacious in transferring the deceased to the sky-world. The use of such raised platforms is practised over a very wide geographical area, and for the reasons given in my pamphlet *The Migrations of Early Culture* (1915).

There can be no doubt that it gives expression to the same belief as the lofty and uncouth funerary beds in Tutankhamen's tomb have forced upon our attention.

Another wave of diffusion of culture is represented in the adoption by European furniture-makers of the Egyptian method of designing legs for chairs, beds and couches. In Egypt itself such a practice can be traced back to the first dynasty 3400 or more b.c. But the lion paws were adopted in Europe as a design for legs of chairs, etc. almost as soon as the Egyptian craft of carpentering and joinery was introduced. Long after the Queen Anne period Chippendale introduced the Chinese variant, the dragon's feet grasping the moon-pearl symbol. But as I explained in *The Evolution of the Dragon* (1919) the dragon is really a blending of Horus's falcon (eagle) and lion into one composite beast.

Thus the study of these couches has revealed the development in Egypt of a very peculiar but distinctive series of symbolic expressions, each of which is so arbitrary and unexpected that one is able to recognize it and refer it to its true source, in whatever part of the world and at whatever historical period it manifests itself. Hence we are able to use the evidence provided by these three distinct aspects of one essential idea to demonstrate different waves of cultural diffusion which spread from Egypt throughout the world both in ancient and modern times.

CHAPTER VIII

THE ETHICS OF DESECRATION

With the awakening of a world-wide interest in the tomb of Tutankhamen there has been a good deal of not altogether relevant discussion about the ethics of desecration, which is none the less unfortunate because it is inspired by ignorance of the real facts of the case. By inflaming feeling it may help to defeat the object everyone concerned is doing his utmost to achieve, that is, to secure the adequate protection and reverent treatment of the dead pharaoh and his fellow-sleepers. Hence it is necessary to put the issue in its true light.

It seems to have been overlooked by those who write about leaving the royal mummies in their own tombs that in the past only one of them was actually found in his own tomb, and that this pharaoh, Amenhotep II, was left there reposing in his own sarcophagus. It is equally important to note that it was Mr Howard Carter, who is in charge of the present work for the late Lord Carnarvon, who was at that time Inspector of Antiquities at Luxor and was largely responsible for this decision. Nor is it any secret that those responsible for the present work propose to leave the mummy of Tutankhamen in the tomb, provided that the risk of damage can be guarded against.

The issue raised by the oft-repeated protests against desecration is complicated by the fact that in every case the mummies of the pharaohs were plundered and grossly maltreated by their own subjects more than thirty centuries ago; and, except in two or three instances, were unceremoniously removed from their own tombs and hidden away in any place that happened to be convenient.

If archæologists did not open and examine these tombs there is no doubt that in time the native tomb-robbers of Luxor, the most experienced members of their craft to be found anywhere, would in time discover the hidden tombs, plundering them and destroying the historical evidence. There can be no question that the work of the archæologist when conscientiously done saves the ancient tombs from wilful destruction and gives the mummies and the furniture a new lease of assured existence. So long as these tombs are left alone there is always the risk that they will be desecrated at any moment.

The problem which the archæologist has to solve, once he has opened a tomb, is what is the proper course to take with reference to the mummies and the funerary equipment. It is claimed by many writers to the Press that at any rate the bodies of the kings ought to be restored.

But even if it were possible to replace the royal mummies in their own tombs, and to persuade the museums of the world to return their sarcophagi and funerary equipment, it would still be a moot point whether such procedures would save them from desecration. For, unless large sums of money are spent in equipping the tombs against the attacks of robbers and providing guards, such measures would defeat the purpose that prompted them. For the mummies would become the lure for the greed of the Theban population, which for sixty centuries and more has been habituated to tomb-robbing, and has shown little respect for the mummies of even the most famous of its rulers. In fact, the most powerful sovereigns of Egypt have suffered worst at the hands of the people of their own metropolis. The mummies of the greatest emperors and wisest statesmen of the eighteenth dynasty, such as Thothmes III and Amenhotep III, were stripped and badly mutilated; and it is more likely than not that the mummy of the famous Hatshepsut, the Queen Elizabeth of Egyptian history, was totally destroyed. Even when Amenhotep II (together with the mummies found with him) were left in his own tomb, it was not long before the tomb was entered by plunderers and wanton damage inflicted on the bodies left in it. In my volume of the Official Catalogue of the Cairo Museum, dealing with the royal mummies, gruesome evidence is given of the mutilation effected upon the bodies of a prince and two princesses in this tomb, both by ancient and modern robbers.

The moral of all this is that unless the tomb is rendered burglar-proof, and in addition is protected by adequate guards, it is inviting desecration to leave the mummies in them. Everyone immediately concerned with the problem of Tutankhamen's mummy agrees that, if it is feasible, it should be left in its own tomb and adequately protected there after a thorough examination of it has been made, and all the information as to age and infirmities which the X-rays can afford has been obtained. The late Lord Carnarvon was strongly in favour of this course of action, and Mr Howard Carter has always been in favour of leaving the mummies in their tombs. But if this is done they must be adequately guarded. For it is not an exaggeration to claim that in the past the removal of the royal mummies to the Cairo Museum saved them from destruction, or from being broken up for disposal to tourists, as in former centuries some of them were sold to druggists. For, as Sir Thomas Browne expressed it two and a half centuries ago, "The Egyptian mummies, which Cambyses or time hath spared, avarice now consumeth. Mummy is become merchandise, Mizraim cures wounds, and Pharaoh is sold for balsams."

But, apart from such considerations, the fact has not received due acknowledgment that the archæologists who are investigating the tomb of Tutankhamen are clearly not engaged in a work of destruction or of desecration, but are striving to preserve his remains and his treasured possessions, and to secure his name and his record from the oblivion which he himself and his representatives strove so hard to avert.

The relatively slight disturbance of the antechamber holds out the prospect that the mummy also may have been spared that wanton destruction which was the fate of so many pharaohs of his dynasty, although it is to be expected that the valuable gold objects upon the body are not likely to have escaped the plunderers.

If the mummy is found, an examination of it by means of the X-rays will be made; but, whatever measures are adopted for wresting from it the story it has to tell, no one need be anxious about its desecration. No damage of any sort will be inflicted upon the body; but every precaution will be taken to assure that prolongation of its existence within its own sarcophagus which the embalmer of thirty-two centuries ago aimed at achieving.

In the commentary on the discoveries in Tutankhamen's tomb I have dealt mainly with aspects of the new revelation of Egyptian customs and beliefs that to most readers may seem less impressive than the dazzling display of artistic treasures which has aroused in them an interest in archæology.

But to the student who is interested in tracing out the origin of the customs and beliefs which have shaped the fabric of civilization and influenced the trends of even our own thoughts, the objective expression of ancient beliefs displayed in Tutankhamen's tomb is the most important outcome of Mr Howard Carter's discovery.

For it enables us to realize more vividly than before the relentless and persistent logic with which the ancient Egyptian theologian strove by any and every device he could think of, to make as certain as any physical or magical procedure could make it, to give a new lease of life or existence to the dead. Many modern scholars object to the use of the word logic to apply to a series of procedures inconsistent the one with the other except in their ultimate aim, and are constantly emphasizing and marvelling at their lack of cogency and consistency. But the modern psychologist has recently been insisting that we ourselves, and, in fact, all mankind, are just as illogical as the Ancient Egyptian priesthood. In our everyday life we are hourly doing things as glaringly inconsistent the one with the other as anything that the Egyptians ever did. It is merely that our wider acquaintance with the nature of matter and the properties of living creatures enables us the more readily to hide our inconsistencies and rationalize our statements so as to hide our ignorance and lack of cogency.

In this connexion it is important to try and put ourselves in the position of the theologians of Tutankhamen's time, and ask whether it is likely that they really imagined the ceremonial couches to be potent to transfer the dead king to the sky. They knew perfectly well that the couches could not effect this physical transference to a topographical heaven. But long usage had accustomed them to attach a definite symbolic meaning to the ceremonial practice of placing the mummy of the king upon such couches. This was supposed to confer upon the dead king immortality and divinity, to identify him with the sun-god Re in the sky.

The problem which is perhaps responsible for most disagreement between Egyptian scholars to-day is the relationship of the two gods Osiris and Re, with both of which the dead king was identified as a means of attaining immortality. The obvious connecting link between them is the rôle assigned to Horus, who, as the son of Osiris, is charged with the function of securing for the dead king the same boons which he was able to confer on Osiris. Yet as a sun-god, intimately associated with Re, Horus could also secure for him the solar heaven and enable him to dwell with Re, if not be identified with him, in the sun.

There is a profound difference of opinion whether Osiris or Re was the earliest god. Philologists like Professor Breasted and Dr Blackman, who derive their knowledge from the literary texts (which, however, were not put into writing until all thought and expression were dominated by the sun-cult and the Pyramid Texts were actually written by Heliopolitan priests) insist on the priority of the sun-god Re.

Ethnologists who know how relatively recent is the belief in a sky-world and in sun-worship insist upon the priority of the god Osiris, who was originally a king on earth. To my mind the whole conception of deity and the attributes of the earliest gods can be understood and explained only if we admit that Osiris was the first god and that Re acquired his reputation secondarily from Osiris.

In Tutankhamen's tomb the one idea that informed the funerary ritual and equipment was this identification with Osiris, and the solar embellishments are clearly additions to the more ancient practices. I have entered in detail into the interesting problems of the funerary couches in order to bring out in a definite and concrete form the essential meaning of the whole equipment of Tutankhamen's tomb.

What renders the obtrusiveness of the Osirian element in Tutankhamen's ritual additionally significant is the fact that he had been a worshipper of the sun's disc, the Aton, and had just been converted to that denomination of the Re-cult which was associated with Amen. But although these different forms of the sun-cult were in turn his confessed beliefs, it is a striking demonstration of the fundamental nature of the Osirian cult that it dominates the ceremonies of Tutankhamen's death and burial.

Printed in Great Britain
by Amazon

39139453R00057